The Flavours Series

SALADS

ELAINE ELLIOT

Photography by Julian Beveridge

FORMAC PUBLISHING COMPANY LIMITED
HALIFAX 1999

PHOTO CREDITS:
All photographs by Julian Beveridge except where noted below:
Dr. Mary Ruth McDonald, Research Scientist, University of Guelph, Dept. of Plant Agriculture, Muck Crops Research Station: p 4, top

PARTICIPATING ESTABLISHMENTS:
The Actor's Retreat Café, Victoria, PEI
The Algonquin, St. Andrews-by-the-Sea, NB
Amherst Shore Country Inn, Lorneville, NS
Arbor View Inn, Lunenburg, NS
Blomidon Inn, Wolfville, NS
Boscawen Inn, Lunenburg, NS
The Briars Resort, Jackson's Point, ON
Charlotte Lane Café & Crafts, Shelburne, NS
Dalvay-by-the-Sea, Dalvay, PEI
The Dunes Café, Brackley Beach, PEI
Haddon Hall Inn, Chester, NS
Halliburton House Inn, Halifax, NS
The Inn at Bay Fortune, Bay Fortune, PEI
Inn on the Cove, Saint John, NB
Inn on the Lake, Waverley, NS

The Innlet Café, Mahone Bay, NS
Libertine Kitchen & Café, Halifax, NS
Little Shemoque Country Inn, Port Elgin, NB
Madelyn's Bistro, Lunenburg, NS
Murray Manor Bed & Breakfast, Yarmouth, NS
The Prince Edward Hotel, Charlottetown, PEI
Seasons in Thyme, Summerside, PEI
Shadow Lawn Country Inn, Rothesay, NB
Shaw's Hotel and Cottages, Brackley Beach, PEI
Sunshine on Main Café & Bistro, Antigonish, NS
Tattingstone Inn, Wolfville, NS
The Whitman Inn, Kempt, NS

This book is dedicated to the many chefs and innkeepers who have generously provided recipes and support and to my patient family.

Formac Publishing Company acknowledges the support of the Department of Canadian Heritage and the Nova Scotia Department of Education and Culture in the development of writing and publishing in Canada.

Canadian Cataloguing in Publication Data
Elliot, Elaine, 1939-
    Salads
    (The Flavours series)
    Includes index.
    ISBN 0-88780-475-6

    1. Salads. I. Title. II. Series
    TX807.E44 1999   641.8'3   C99-950061-9

Formac Publishing Company Limited
5502 Atlantic Street
Halifax, N.S.
B3H 1G4

Distribution in the United States:
Seven Hills Book Distributors
1531 Tremont Street
Cincinnati, OH 45214

CONTENTS

INTRODUCTION

To continue with the theme of the successful Flavour Series of cookbooks, I have decided to introduce you to the wonderful ways in which our chefs make salads into culinary masterpieces. These artfully presented creations represent what I consider the new emerging Canadian cuisine. In this book you will find a mosaic of dishes, each salad being as unique as its creator.

As in the past, these recipes are supplied by chefs of selected inns and restaurants, plus a few from my personal collection.

Photographer Julian Beveridge has visited many of the dining rooms, capturing the salads as they are served. Each recipe has been tested and adjusted to serve four to six persons.

VARIETIES

Ah, the wonders of salad greens! Romaine, leaf, red oak, Boston, and iceberg lettuce, radicchio, spinach, endive...the list is endless. Each variety offers a distinctive taste and texture and when combined, provide unlimited opportunities for decorative presentation.

We all love the "freshly picked" flavour of in-season local greens, but you need to develop a rapport with the produce manager in your local supermarket so that you can get good advice about imported varieties during the winter months. Ask if anyone is producing hydroponic lettuces. Grown in water in green-houses, without soil, pesticides, insecticides or herbicides, these lettuces are extremely clean. Varieties may include Boston, Bibb, red or green oak and while they keep very well when wrapped in plastic and refrigerated, for optimum flavour, use them close to time of purchase.

CARE

Salad greens should be gently rinsed, spun dry or blotted dry with paper towel and stored in zip-locked bags in the crisper section of the refrigerator. Greens purchased in air tight packaging should be refrigerated "as is" and rinsed just before serving. Remember, greens should be torn, not cut, into bite-sized pieces and any large stems should be removed.

Purchase your salad greens close to the time you plan to serve them. As a rule, iceberg and romaine will keep up to a week, spinach three to four days, but tender baby greens such as the popular mesclun mixes keep only one or two days.

NUTRITIONAL VALUE

Canada's guide to healthy eating suggests five to ten servings of fruits and vegetables each day. A one cup serving of salad greens combined with two or more half-cup servings of fruits or vegetables takes you well on the way to fulfilling these requirements.

Nutrients in salad greens vary, although the darker green they are, the better. A one-cup serving of torn spinach leaves contains 12.3 calories, one cup serving of romaine, 9.1 calories and an equal serving of buttercrunch lettuce 7.4 calories. All are good sources of Vitamins A and C.

EDIBLE FLOWERS AND HERBS

Many of these recipes call for the addition of edible flowers, and while their use is considered somewhat 'nouvelle cuisine,' I remind you that flowers have been used in food preparation since the time of the early Romans!

Flowers and herbs that are to be used in food preparation must be grown without the use of pesticides or insecticides. I also caution that they not be grown in containers made of pressurized woods. These materials contain toxic chemicals which leach into the soil and thus into the plant. For my personal use, I grow my edible flowers and herbs in large clay pots situated in an area away from the possible contamination of garden or lawn sprays.

The list is endless, but to get you started on the delights of edible flowers I suggest individual geranium flowers, whole violets, johnny-jump-ups, pansies, or periwinkle flowers plus apple or plum blossoms. Later in the season you may harvest bee balm, calendula, marigold or chive petals, nasturtium flowers and leaves. For an elegant presentation, why not try rose or tulip petals!

THE DRESSED SALAD

The secret of a good dressing is to use the best quality oils and vinegars available, and to dress the salad lightly, just before serving. What you add to the salad is a personal choice — absolutely anything goes. If you like mushrooms and loathe tomatoes, toss mushrooms into your salad instead of tomatoes. Add cheese, crumbled pieces of crisp bacon, hard-boiled egg wedges, whatever you fancy. So, off to the market you go. armed with this array of recipes you will never again reach for the commercially bottled salad dressing. Bon Appetit!

THE FIRST COURSE

*G*reens, greens, everywhere beautiful greens! In this section you can experience a variety of salads, from the classic Greek Salad from Shaw's Hotel and Cottages to a Caesar with a seafood twist, the creation of the chef at Actor's Retreat Café.

◄ *Five Lettuce and Edible Flower Salad with Black Currant Vinaigrette from The Whitman Inn, Kempt, NS.*

FIVE LETTUCE AND EDIBLE FLOWERS SALAD WITH BLACK CURRANT VINAIGRETTE

THE WHITMAN INN, KEMPT, NS

Nancy and Bruce Gurnham grow most of their own lettuce and flowers in the inn's extensive gardens. Having the ingredients on hand allows them to be inventive and change their menus with the seasons. In spring they use chive florets, pansies and johnny-jump-ups, later in the summer, lemon and tangerine marigolds, thyme and oregano blossoms — all individually plucked.

Assorted lettuces to serve 4, e.g., romaine, black seeded Simpson, green and red oak leaf, buttercrunch

4 calendula flowers

4 bee balm flowers

24 borage blossoms*

Black Currant Vinaigrette (Recipe follows)

Prepare lettuce leaves and divide between four chilled salad plates, taking care to arrange a variety of colours and textures between each serving.

Sprinkle each salad with the petals of a calendula and bee balm flower, and ring the plates with borage flowers, leaving one for the centre of the plate. Drizzle with Black Currant Vinaigrette. Serves 4.

* To remove the blossom from the borage stem gently grasp the stem in one hand and gently pinch out and separate the blue part from the stem part.

Black Currant Vinaigrette

This recipe is the creation of chef John Theiss, brother of innkeeper Nancy Gurnham. He suggests you use homemade mayonnaise or a good quality egg-based mayonnaise.

1/3 cup red wine vinegar

1/3 cup extra virgin olive oil

2/3 cup canola oil

1 large clove garlic, minced

2–2 1/2 tablespoons black currant concentrate

1–2 tablespoons mayonnaise

several grindings of fresh black pepper

Whisk together all ingredients until well blended. Keep chilled until serving time. Yields 1 1/2 cups dressing.

GREEK SALAD

SHAW'S HOTEL AND COTTAGES,
BRACKLEY BEACH, PEI

This is the classic version served with kalamata olives, feta cheese and an oregano infused dressing.

romaine lettuce to serve four

1 small purple onion, cut in rings

2 tomatoes, cut in wedges

1/2 cup Greek Kalamata olives

1/2 English cucumber, peeled, seeded and cut into sticks

1/4 pound feta cheese, crumbled

Shaw's Greek Salad Dressing, recipe follows.

To assemble salads, arrange prepared romaine, onion rings, tomato wedges, olives, cucumber pieces and crumbled cheese on four chilled salad plates. Drizzle with dressing. Serves 4.

Shaw's Greek Salad Dressing

1 cup egg-based mayonnaise

1 garlic clove, crushed

3 tablespoons raspberry vinegar

1 teaspoon fresh thyme, chopped or 1/4 teaspoon dry

1 teaspoon fresh oregano, chopped or 1/4 teaspoon dry

1/2 teaspoon Worcestershire sauce

Combine dressing ingredients in a blender or food processor and chill until ready to serve. Yields 1 1/4 cup dressing.

POTATO PEAR SALAD

INN ON THE LAKE, WAVERLEY, NS

Chef Helmut Pflueger marries the subtle flavours of pears and potatoes in this innovative salad which he serves either warm or chilled.

4–5 medium potatoes, scrubbed

1/4 cup vegetable oil

1 1/2 tablespoons cider vinegar

3/4 teaspoon salt

1/4 teaspoon freshly ground pepper

2 medium-sized pears

1 head romaine lettuce

In a large saucepan cover potatoes with water and bring to a boil. Reduce heat to low, cover and cook until potatoes are fork-tender, approximately 25–30 minutes. Drain, set aside until cool enough to handle.

While potatoes are cooking, whisk together the oil, vinegar, salt and pepper. Set aside.

Peel potatoes and cut into 1/8-inch slices. Core and thinly slice pears. Gently toss potato and pear slices in dressing until well coated.

To serve, spoon potatoes and pears into a salad bowl lined with lettuce leaves. Serve warm or chilled.

Yields 4 servings.

BOSCAWEN INN'S CAESAR SALAD

BOSCAWEN INN, LUNENBURG, NS

There are times when the simplest of salads are the most flavourful. I have tried many Caesar recipes and this is one of the best! At the Boscawen Inn it is served with warm garlic bread.

1 large head romaine, rinsed and torn into bite-sized pieces

1 cup good quality egg-based mayonnaise

1–2 small garlic cloves, finely minced

1 1/2 tablespoons capers, drained and chopped

1/3 teaspoon dry mustard

2 1/2 teaspoons white wine

1 teaspoons lemon juice

Croutons and grated parmesan cheese, for garnish

Prepare romaine and place in a large salad bowl. Whisk together mayonnaise, garlic, capers and dry mustard. Stir in wine and lemon juice and refrigerate several hours to allow flavours to blend.

To serve, drizzle dressing over salad greens, toss and serve. Garnish salads with croutons and grated parmesan cheese.

Seasoned Croutons *(Supplied by author)*

6 slices day-old white bread

1/4 cup olive oil

1/8 teaspoon garlic powder

3 tablespoons grated parmesan cheese

Preheat oven to 300° F. Brush both side of bread with oil, sprinkle with garlic and parmesan cheese. Cut into 3/4 inch cubes and bake on a cookie sheet for 30 minutes, stirring once. Cool, then store in an air-tight container. Yields 2 cups.

Caesar Salad as served at Lunenburg's Boscawen Inn ▶

ORANGE ALMOND SALAD

SUNSHINE ON MAIN CAFÉ & BISTRO, ANTIGONISH, NS

*In this delicious salad chef Mark Gabrieau serves generous portions
of mandarin orange segments, raisins and roasted nuts. He suggest that sun-dried
cranberries may replace the raisins and that pistachios may replace the almonds.*

mixed salad greens to serve 4

1 can mandarin orange segments, drained,
10-ounce size

1 large tomato, diced, optional

1/3 cup raisins

4 tablespoons toasted almonds

several sprigs fresh parsley, chopped

freshly ground black pepper

Sunshine Café Dressing, recipe follows

Divide prepared greens between 4 salad
plates. Arrange orange segments and tomato
on top of salads. Sprinkle with raisins,
almonds, parsley and pepper. Drizzle with
Sunshine Café Dressing. Serves 4.

Sunshine Café Dressing

zest and juice of 1 lemon

1 cup heavy cream (35% m.f.)

1/2 teaspoon ground ginger

pinch of salt

pinch of black pepper

1 tablespoon raspberry or sherry vinegar

Remove zest from lemon and finely dice.
Halve lemon, remove juice and set aside.
In a mixing bowl combine all ingredients
and whip lightly until the consistency of a
creamy dressing.

What a wonderful combination of fruits and nuts in chef Mark Gabrieau's Orange Almond Salad ▶

CHARLOTTE'S MESCLUN SALAD

CHARLOTTE LANE CAFÉ & CRAFTS, SHELBURNE, NS

"Pretty as a picture" would describe chef Roland Glauser's refreshing mesclun salad. This is one of the many innovative dishes served at this little restaurant and gift shop located on a tiny Shelburne side street aptly called Charlotte Lane.

1/3 cup raspberry vinegar

1 teaspoon Dijon mustard

1/4 cup liquid honey

a few drops Worcestershire sauce, or to taste

1 cup extra virgin olive oil

mesclun salad mix to serve 4

Caramelized Garlic, recipe follows

Spicy Walnuts, recipe follows

6–8 dried apricots, finely sliced

edible flower blossoms*, as garnish

Combine vinegar, mustard, honey and Worcestershire sauce in a food processor or blender and mix. With machine running, add oil in a slow stream until mixture is emulsified.

To serve, toss crisp mesclun mix with dressing and divide between 4 salad plates. Top salads with caramelized garlic segments, walnuts, finely sliced apricots and edible flower blossoms. Serves 4.

* For information about edible flower blossoms see introduction.

Caramelized Garlic

1–2 garlic bulb

1 cup red wine

1/4 cup balsamic vinegar

6 tablespoons sugar

Divide and peel garlic into cloves. Combine with wine, vinegar and sugar and simmer until garlic is very soft and mixture starts to caramelize, approximately 30 minutes. Remove from burner and cool.

Spicy Walnuts

2–3 tablespoons olive oil

1 cup walnut pieces

1/2 teaspoon salt

1/2 teaspoon pepper

1/4 teaspoon paprika

1/8 teaspoon cayenne

1/4 teaspoon curry

In a skillet heat oil over medium setting. Add walnut pieces, sprinkle liberally with spices and sauté until lightly roasted. Cool to room temperature and reserve. Yields 1 cup.

Chef Roland Glauser and his wife Kathleen aptly named this decorative salad Charlotte's Mesclun Salad after the tiny lane where their restaurant is located in Shelburne, NS ▶

WILD NEW BRUNSWICK BLUEBERRIES WITH NASTURTIUM LEAVES AND FLOWERS

THE ALGONQUIN, ST. ANDREWS-BY-THE-SEA, NB

Chef Willie White prepares this colourful salad using albino blueberries and golden raspberries. In testing I found regular berries worked as well.

1 head butter leaf lettuce

20 nasturtium leaves

1 head Belgian endive

1/2 cup blueberries

1/2 cup raspberries

4 stalks fresh chives

dressing, recipe follows

12 nasturtium flowers, as garnish

Rinse and dry greens and flowers. Cut endive into strips and tie a small bunch with a chive. Place greens on 4 salad plates with a bunch of endive standing in the middle. Sprinkle the blueberries and raspberries around the plate. Drizzle with dressing and garnish with nasturtium flowers. Serves 4.

Dressing

2 egg yolks

1 teaspoon dry mustard

4 tablespoons balsamic vinegar

6 tablespoons canola oil

6 tablespoons heavy cream (35% m.f.)

salt and freshly ground pepper, to taste

In a blender combine yolks, mustard and vinegar. With machine running, add oil in a steady stream and process until emulsified. While machine continues to run, add cream and mix only until combined. Season with salt and freshly ground pepper, refrigerate. Yields 1 cup dressing.

PEARS GLAZED IN PORT ON A MEDLEY OF GREENS

THE PRINCE EDWARD HOTEL, CHARLOTTETOWN, PEI

Gorgonzola cheese and pears are a marvellous combination. At the Prince Edward Hotel chef Paul Paboudjian poaches his pears to a beautiful deep pink colour. On the plate, the salad is a work of art!

4 large pears, peeled

3 cup sweet port

1 cup Gorgonzola cheese, crumbled

4 cups mesclun mix or a variety of greens

dressing, recipe follows

additional Gorgonzola, crumbled as garnish

8–12 sprigs fresh basil and chive shoots, as garnish

Stand pears in a deep saucepan and cover with port. Bring to a simmer and cook until pears are tender, approximately 10–15 minutes. Remove from burner and cool, being careful that the pears have been totally submerged on all sides while in the liquid.

Remove cooled pears from liquid and cut off the tops approximately 1 1/2-inches from the stem; hollow out the bottom half with a mellow baller. Stuff cavities with cheese and set aside.

To serve, arrange salad greens attractively on four salad plates. Top with poached pears, leaning the top of the pear against the side of the fruit. Crumble additional Gorgonzola over greens and drizzle with dressing. Garnish with basil and chive shoots.

Dressing

1/2 cup extra virgin olive oil

1/3 cup apple cider

3 tablespoons pure maple syrup

2 teaspoons Dijon mustard

salt and pepper, to taste

In a stainless steel bowl whisk oil, cider, syrup and mustard until emulsified. Season with salt and pepper. Yields 1 cup.

GREEN SALAD WITH "TIDES TABLE" DRESSING

INN ON THE COVE, SAINT JOHN, NB

Willa and Ross Mavis are busy innkeepers. Not only do they run a delightful establishment on the shores of the Bay of Fundy, but have written their own cookbook, Tides Table, and host a TV cooking show. Ross states that honey and cider vinegar are the perfect foil for the salty bite of anchovy paste in this unique dressing.

6 cups fresh salad greens

1/4 cup liquid honey

1/4 cup apple cider vinegar

2 teaspoons dry mustard

1 tablespoon onion, grated

1/4 teaspoon salt

4 teaspoons anchovy paste

2/3 cup virgin olive oil

2 teaspoons poppy seeds

1 small red onion, finely sliced

Wash and freshen salad greens in cold water. Spin dry.

In a blender or food processor combine honey, vinegar, mustard, onion, salt and anchovy paste. With blender running add olive oil in a thin stream until well mixed. Add poppy seeds, stir to incorporate and chill for about 30 minutes before using.

Toss salad greens and red onion with just enough dressing to lightly coat. Pile salad decoratively on plate and drizzle a little more dressing onto salad and plate as accent. Serves 4–6.

MARITIME CAESAR

THE ACTOR'S RETREAT CAFÉ, VICTORIA, PEI

Erskine Smith, artistic director of PEI's Victoria Playhouse shared this Caesar Salad recipe with innkeeper Pam Stevenson. It has become a house favourite.

1 large head romaine lettuce

2 egg yolks

3 ounces smoked herring fillet

2 garlic cloves, crushed

1 tablespoon Worcestershire sauce

juice of 1/2 small lemon

1/3 cup Balsamic vinegar

2/3 cup green olive oil

1/2 cup grated parmesan cheese

toasted croutons, as garnish

additional parmesan cheese, as garnish

Rinse and dry romaine lettuce and tear into bite-sized pieces. Place in a large salad bowl.

In a separate bowl, blend together egg yolks, herring fillet and garlic with wooden spoon. Whisk in Worcestershire sauce, lemon juice, vinegar and oil and blend well. Stir in cheese, mixing until fully blended.

Drizzle lettuce with dressing and serve with toasted croutons and additional cheese as garnish. Serves 4.

A Caesar with a nautical flavour, Maritime Caesar ▶ from the Actor's Retreat Café, Victoria, PEI

BOSCAWEN INN'S HOUSE SALAD

BOSCAWEN INN, LUNENBURG, NS

Innkeeper Ann O'Dowd uses a variety of three different lettuces of different colours and textures. Combined with garden fresh vegetables, the salad is a delight to behold.

lettuce to serve 4 (leaf, iceberg, Boston or romaine)

2 tomatoes, cut in wedges

1/2 red pepper, in julienne strips

2–3 large white mushrooms, sliced

1/2 English style cucumber, sliced

alfalfa sprouts

mandarin orange segments

Boscawen House Dressing, recipe follows

Prepare lettuces and divide between four chilled serving plates. Arrange tomato wedges, pepper, mushrooms and cucumber over greens. Top with alfalfa sprouts and a few orange segments. Drizzle with Boscawen House Dressing. Serves 4.

Boscawen House Dressing

The chef at Boscawen uses only good quality egg based mayonnaise in this dressing. In testing, I used Hellman's brand with great success.

2 cups egg-based mayonnaise

1/3 cup sugar

3 tablespoons liquid honey

2 tablespoons white wine

1 tablespoon lemon juice

1/3 cup heavy cream (35% m.f.)

2 1/2 teaspoons dill paste or dried dill weed

1 teaspoon powdered thyme

1/2 teaspoon curry

1 tablespoon steak spice

In a bowl whisk together the mayonnaise, sugar, honey, wine and lemon juice. In a saucepan, over medium heat, combine cream, dill paste, thyme, curry and steak spice until dill paste has dissolved. Remove from heat, cool and stir into mayonnaise mixture. Refrigerate. Yields 2 1/2 cups dressing.

Only at Lunenburg's Boscawen Inn will you find the distinctive flavour of ▶ this dill-enhanced Boscawen House Salad

MIXED GREEN SALAD WITH SCENTED MAPLE WALNUT VINAIGRETTE

HADDON HALL INN, CHESTER, NS

Even the early Romans used edible flowers in their food presentation, so be as adventurous as the chef at Haddon Hall when you decorate your salad plate.

mixed salad greens to serve 4

English-style cucumber, sliced

2 large tomatoes, cut in wedges

edible flowers, e.g., chives, pansies, nasturtiums

Maple Walnut Vinaigrette (recipe follows)

Rinse and thoroughly dry greens, then refrigerate until ready to serve. Rim the salad plates with cucumber, pile greens in the centre and top with 3 or 4 tomato wedges. Garnish with nasturtiums, chives and assorted flower petals.

Drizzle with Maple Walnut Vinaigrette.

Serves 4.

Maple Walnut Vinaigrette

1/4 cup walnut vinegar

2 tablespoons maple syrup

salt and pepper, to taste

1 cup extra virgin olive oil

Whisk together the vinegar and maple syrup. Season with salt and pepper and slowly pour in the oil while continuing to whisk until ingredients are emulsified. Yields 1 1/4 cups dressing.

MURRAY MANOR ORIENTAL SALAD

MURRAY MANOR BED AND BREAKFAST, YARMOUTH, NS

Innkeeper Joan Semple has found that toasted sesame seeds and soya sauce gives this salad an oriental flavour.

assorted lettuce greens to serve 4

1 large tomato, cut in wedges

1/2 English-style cucumber, sliced

4 large mushrooms, sliced

1/2 red pepper, in julienne strips

Oriental Salad Dressing, recipe follows

1 cup alfalfa sprouts

1/4 cup sesame seeds, toasted

In a large salad bowl combine lettuce, tomato, cucumber, mushrooms and red peppers. Drizzle with Oriental Salad Dressing and toss. Divide salads between 4 serving plates. Sprinkle with alfalfa sprouts and toasted sesame seeds.

Oriental Salad Dressing

1/2 small onion, minced

1-2 garlic cloves, minced

1/4 cup + 2 teaspoons soya sauce

1 1/2 cup vegetable oil

2 1/2 tablespoons lemon juice

Using a food processor or blender process all ingredients until emulsified. Store any unused dressing in refrigerator up to 1 week. Yields 2 cups dressing.

Haddon Hall's Mixed Green Salad with Scented Maple Vinaigrette ▶
melds a greens assortment with a delicate dressing

GERMAN-STYLE WARM POTATO SALAD

LIBERTINE CAFÉ AND KITCHEN, HALIFAX, NS

Chef Peter Woodworth credits this recipe to his wife Sandra who brought this family favourite from her home in Germany. Cornichons used in the recipe are tart pickles, often called gherkins.

5 medium russet potatoes

5 eggs, hard boiled

8 cornichons, chopped into a small dice

small bunch chives, chopped

1 tablespoon Dijon mustard

1/2 cup vegetable oil

1/4 cup white wine vinegar

salt and pepper, to taste

Scrub potatoes and place, skin on, in a pot of cold water. Bring to a boil, reduce heat and cook until potatoes are barely fork tender. Remove from burner, drain and cut into bite-sized pieces. Cover to keep warm.

Remove shells from hard boiled eggs and slice in half. Remove yolks and set aside. Chop egg whites into bite-sized pieces and place in bowl with potatoes. Add chopped cornichons and chives.

Place mustard in a large salad bowl. Press egg yolks through a sieve and add to the mustard. Using a whisk, gradually incorporate oil into mustard mixture, stir in vinegar and season with salt and pepper. Place potatoes, egg white pieces, pickles and chives in bowl of dressing and toss lightly. Serve warm.

Yields 4 servings.

Well worth the preparation time, Chef Peter Woodworth's authentic German-Style Warm ▶ Potato Salad was prepared at Libertine Café and Kitchen, Halifax, NS

FRENCH HONEY SALAD

INNLET CAFÉ, MAHONE BAY, NS

Oh, this is a "honey" of a salad! Owner-chef Jack Sorenson warns that this dressing tends to separate and must be well shaken or stirred before serving.

1/2 cup toasted unblanched almonds, as garnish

2 tomatoes, sliced

1 head romaine, rinsed and in bite-sized pieces

1/2 carrot, thinly sliced

2 stalks celery, sliced

8 radish, sliced

1/2 English-style cucumber, sliced

alfalfa sprouts, as garnish

French Honey Dressing, recipe follows

Preheat oven to 300°F.

Toss almonds with 2 teaspoons French Honey Dressing and spread on a cookie sheet. Toast in oven, stirring frequently, 3–5 minutes. Remove from oven, cool and then crush slightly.

Place tomato slices around the rim of 4 salad plates. In a large bowl combine romaine, carrot, celery, radish and cucumber. Drizzle with French Honey Dressing and toss lightly. Divide between the 4 plates. Top each salad with sprouts and garnish with toasted almond pieces. Serves 4.

French Honey Dressing

1/3 cup liquid honey

1/4 cup freshly squeezed lemon juice

2 teaspoons lemon zest

1/2 teaspoon crushed celery seed

3/4 teaspoon salt

1/2 teaspoon Worcestershire sauce

1/4 teaspoon paprika

1/4 teaspoon dry mustard

1/4 teaspoon ground pepper

3/4 cup vegetable oil

Using a food processor or blender combine all ingredients, except the oil. With machine running, add oil in a steady stream and process until emulsified. Shake or stir well before using. Yields 1 1/4 cups.

This is a honey of a recipe – French Honey Salad as served by chef Jack Sorenson of ▶ Mahone Bay's Innlet Café

THE ACTOR'S RETREAT HOUSE SALAD

THE ACTOR'S RETREAT CAFÉ, VICTORIA, PEI

Pam Stevenson of the Actor's Retreat Café states that this salad dressing must be made with her mom's homemade mayonnaise. We are fortunate that her mom, Hughena, was willing to share her secret recipe!

red and green leaf lettuce to serve 4

2 large tomatoes, cut in wedges

9–12 radishes, sliced

1/2 red onion, thinly sliced and broken into rings

1/2 English-style cucumber, sliced

12 black olives

Actor's Retreat House Dressing, recipe follows

Arrange greens on 4 salad plates. Top with vegetables and drizzle with House Dressing. Serves 4.

Actor's Retreat House Dressing

1/2 cup balsamic vinegar

1/4 cup Hughena's Home-made Mayonnaise (recipe follows)

1/2 cup olive oil

3 tablespoons fresh dill weed (1 tablespoon dried)

3 tablespoons lemon juice

2 tablespoons sugar

Whisk together all ingredients and refrigerate, storing no longer than two days. Shake well before serving. Yields 1 cup.

Hughena's Home-made Mayonnaise

2 eggs

1 cup white sugar

2 tablespoons flour

1 tablespoon dry mustard

1/2 teaspoon salt

1 cup milk

3/4 cup vinegar

In a large mixing bowl, beat eggs. In a separate bowl, mix together the sugar, flour, dry mustard and salt, then sift over eggs. Beat together until foamy. Stir in milk and vinegar.

Place mixture in the top of a double boiler over simmering water. Cook until thickened, approximately 20 minutes, stirring occasionally. Refrigerate. Yields 2 cups.

Two recipes in one. The Actor's Retreat House Salad features a homemade mayonnaise ▶ which is used in this special house dressing

SPINACH AND ORANGE SALAD WITH POPPY SEED DRESSING

CHARLOTTE LANE CAFÉ & CRAFTS, SHELBURNE, NS

Owner-chef Roland Glauser of the Charlotte Lane notes that this is a very versatile salad. The apple and orange segments may be replaced by mango chunks, peach or plum slices, and toasted almonds or pine nuts may be sprinkled on top.

12 ounces fresh spinach, rinsed, dried and large stems removed

1 large Granny Smith apple, diced

1 orange, peeled and sliced

Poppy Seed Dressing, recipe follows

Tear prepared spinach leaves into bite-sized pieces and place in a large salad bowl. Top with apple and orange slices, drizzle with dressing and toss. Refrigerate any remaining dressing for up to 5 days.

Serves 4-6.

Poppy Seed Dressing

1/2 cup liquid honey

1 teaspoon Dijon mustard

1/2 cup fresh orange juice

1/4 cup balsamic vinegar

1/2 cup virgin olive oil

1/4 teaspoon ground sage

2 teaspoons poppy seeds

Whisk together honey, mustard, orange juice, vinegar, oil, sage and poppy seeds. Yields 1 1/2 cups.

Spinach and Orange Salad is a specialty of the Charlotte Lane Café in Shelburne, NS ▶

MAKE AHEAD SALADS

*T*hese salads will become the mainstay of the busy cooks collection. Insalada Verde from Rothesay's Shadow Lawn Country Inn calls for an interesting variety of fresh green vegetables, yet can be prepared early in the day. Pasta Salad from Blomidon Inn improves with a few hours to marinate.

◀ *A variety of vibrant green vegetables makes up Insalada Verde from Shadow Lawn, Rothesay, NB*

INSALADA VERDE

SHADOW LAWN INN, ROTHESAY, NB

Chef Patricia Bullock suggests that the secret to this salad is to use the very freshest vegetables available. Blanch the vegetables several hours in advance and toss with dressing just before serving.

1 1/2 teaspoons salt

1 bunch broccoli, cut in fleurettes

1/2 pound fresh green beans

1 bunch small asparagus spears

1/2 pound snow peas

1/2 pound fresh shelled peas

zest of 1 lemon, finely slivered

1/4 cup orange juice

1/4 cup freshly squeezed lemon juice

3 tablespoons sugar

1/2 cup canola oil

1 teaspoon dried marjoram

1 teaspoon dried oregano

Cut all vegetables into bite-sized pieces, keeping the vegetables separated.

Bring a large pot of water to the boil, add salt. Blanch vegetables separately, allowing 2–3 minutes for the broccoli and green beans, 1 minute for the asparagus and 30 seconds for the snow peas and fresh peas. As each group of vegetables are blanched, immediately remove to a bowl of ice water. Drain cooled vegetables and toss with lemon zest, then refrigerate.

In a small bowl whisk together the orange juice, lemon juice, sugar, oil, marjoram and oregano. Make dressing several hours in advance to allow flavours to blend.

To serve, toss chilled vegetable with a little dressing and arrange on 6 individual salad plates.

WILD RICE SALAD WITH PEARS AND CRANBERRIES

TATTINGSTONE INN, WOLFVILLE, NS

Wild rice has a nutty flavour and Catherine Metzger of Tattingstone Inn developed this delightful recipe to serve as an appetizer. The salad should be prepared early in the day to allow flavours to blend. It is served on a bed of baby greens.

1 cup wild rice

5 cups chicken stock

2 tablespoons olive oil

3 firm pears, cored, peeled and in small dice

zest of one orange, finely sliced

1/4 cup dried cranberries, finely chopped

1/2 cup blanched almonds, toasted

1/3 cup orange juice

1 1/2 tablespoon cider vinegar

2 scallions, green part only, sliced

1/4 cup olive oil (2nd amount)

salt and freshly ground pepper, to taste

baby salad greens to serve 4

Thoroughly rinse rice in cold water. Bring stock to a boil over high heat. Reduce to a simmer and stir in wild rice. Cook rice, loosely covered, for 1 hour or until tender.

Drain to discard any excess liquid and set aside. Heat 2 tablespoons of the olive oil over medium heat and sauté pears for 8 minutes, stirring frequently. Stir pears, zest, cranberries and almonds into rice.

In a small bowl combine orange juice, vinegar and scallions; add oil in a thin stream and whisk constantly until dressing emulsifies. Toss with rice, season with salt and pepper.

Serve at room temperature on a bed of baby salad greens. Serves 4.

SLICED CUCUMBERS WITH CREAMY DRESSING

AMHERST SHORE COUNTRY INN, LORNEVILLE, NS

The prolific gardens at the Amherst Shore Country Inn supply the freshest ingredients for this delightful make-ahead salad.

1 English-style cucumber, unpeeled and thinly sliced

1 1/2 teaspoons salt

1 cup heavy cream (35% m.f.)

2 tablespoons egg-based mayonnaise

1 teaspoon lemon juice

1/4 cup minced chives

Fresh young spinach leaves to serve 6

Prepare cucumber slices and sprinkle with salt, cover and refrigerate several hours.

At serving time whip cream until stiff peaks form. Gently fold in mayonnaise and lemon juice.

To serve, arrange spinach leaves on 6 salad plates. Distribute drained cucumber slices over the spinach and drizzle with dressing. Sprinkle with chives.

Serves 6.

WALDORF SALAD

This recipe was shared by a Nova Scotian innkeeper many years ago. It is an excellent choice to serve during those times of year when traditional salad ingredients are out of season or perhaps not at their prime.

1/2 cup celery, diced

2 teaspoons minced green onion

2 tart Granny Smith apples, peeled and thinly sliced

1/2 cup walnut halves

2 ounces blue cheese, crumbled

1/2 cup egg-based mayonnaise

1/2 cup crème fraîche, sour cream or unflavoured yogurt

assorted lettuce leaves

In a medium bowl combine celery, onions, apples, walnut halves and crumbled cheese.

Whisk together mayonnaise and crème fraîche. Add to the bowl and toss gently to mix and chill.

To serve, divide lettuce between 4 salad plates and top with blue cheese mixture.

Crisp Sliced Cucumbers with a Creamy Dressing as presented by ▶
innkeeper Donna Lacoby, Amherst Shore Country Inn

CHILLED PASTA SALAD WITH ROASTED EGGPLANT

THE WHITMAN INN, KEMPT, NS

This is a versatile recipe, using the freshest of herbs from the inn's gardens.
If fresh herbs are unavailable, use one teaspoon each of dried herbs

2 pounds eggplant, in 1/2-inch slices

salt

1/2 cup olive oil

1 tablespoon fresh basil, chopped

1 tablespoon fresh oregano, chopped

1 tablespoon fresh thyme, chopped

2 garlic cloves, minced

1 pound radiatore or penne pasta, cooked
al dente

1 1/2 cups Kalamata olives, pitted and sliced

2 or 3 ripe tomatoes, chopped or 1 can diced
tomatoes, drained (28-ounce size)

4–6 cloves garlic, minced

1/4 cup fresh Italian parsley, chopped

1/4 cup red wine vinegar

1/4 cup capers, drained

generous grinding of fresh black pepper

salt, to taste

red chili pepper flakes, to taste

1/4 cup grated mozzarella cheese, optional

Clean and slice eggplant, sprinkle with salt
and let stand in a colander for 1/2 hour.

Combine oil, basil, oregano, thyme and 2
garlic cloves in a small bowl. Gently wipe
eggplant slices dry and brush with oil mixture.
Reserve remaining oil.

Preheat oven to 350°F. Place eggplant on a
baking sheet and roast until tender and
slightly blackened. Let cool, then slice into
strips 1/2-inch wide by 1 1/2-inches long.

Prepare pasta, drain and set aside. In a bowl
combine reserved oil mixture, olives,
tomatoes, additional garlic, Italian parsley,
vinegar and capers. Season with salt, pepper
and chili flakes. Gently toss together pasta,
eggplant and dressing. Sprinkle with grated
cheese, if desired. Serve chilled.

Yields 6–8 servings.

Chilled Pasta salad with Roasted Eggplant as served at Whitman Inn, Kempt, NS ▶

BLOMIDON INN PASTA SALAD

THE BLOMIDON INN, WOLFVILLE, NS

In this pasta salad with a Mediterranean flair, chef Sean Laceby uses plump Italian or "Roma" plum tomatoes, black olives, peppers and roasted tomatoes to accent the inn's fresh pasta.

1/2 pound fresh rotini, cooked al dente

1/4 cup balsamic vinegar

1/4–1/3 cup virgin olive oil

2 small garlic cloves, minced

1/2 each small red, green and yellow peppers, in small chunks

4 Italian plum tomatoes, diced

1/2 cup roasted Roma tomatoes, recipe follows

5 ounces feta cheese, crumbled

3/4 cup pitted black olives

1 tablespoon fresh thyme, chopped

2 tablespoons fresh parsley, chopped

2 tablespoons fresh oregano, chopped

salt and pepper, to taste

Cook pasta until al dente. Drain and cool.

Place vinegar in a bowl and whisk in oil. Add garlic, peppers, fresh and roasted tomatoes, olives and herbs. Season with salt and pepper and toss with chilled pasta.

Serves 4–6.

Roasted Roma Tomatoes

6 plum tomatoes, cut in wedges

1 tablespoon puréed oven roasted garlic, recipe follows

1 teaspoon fresh thyme, minced

1 1/2 teaspoons fresh basil, minced

1 teaspoon fresh oregano, minced

1 1/2 tablespoons balsamic vinegar

1 tablespoon olive oil

salt and pepper, to taste

Combine all ingredients in a bowl and marinate 1 hour. Drain and roast on a baking sheet at 250°F for 4 hours.

Oven Roasted Garlic *(supplied by author)*

Preheat oven to 325°F.

Lightly coat one whole unpeeled garlic bulb or individual unpeeled cloves with a little olive oil and bake until browned and softened. Allow approximately 30 minutes for the cloves and 45 minutes for the whole garlic bulb. Gently squeeze garlic out of its peel with your fingers.

A Mediterranean flair is evident in the Blomidon Inn Pasta Salad ▶

MAIN COURSE SALADS

usy schedule? Take a tip from our chefs and prepare a filling salad. When served with crusty bread or rolls, these offerings are substantial and sure to please!

◄ Chicken Sesmae Salad from the Dunes Café, Brackley Beach, PEI.

THE DUNES CAFÉ CHICKEN SESAME SALAD

THE DUNES CAFÉ,
BRACKLEY BEACH, PEI

The Dunes chef Shaun McKay tosses this salad of baby greens with deliciously sesame infused chicken pieces and his rendition of Sesame Soy Dressing.

baby salad greens to serve 4

4 boneless chicken breasts, 4 ounces each

1/2 cup sesame seeds

2–3 tablespoons sesame oil

Sesame Soy Dressing (recipe follows)

Rinse and dry salad greens and divide between four serving plates. Slice chicken breasts into 1/2-inch strips and dredge chicken in sesame seeds. Over medium high heat, sauté chicken in oil until cooked, approximately 3–4 minutes. Arrange chicken strips over salad greens and drizzle with Sesame Soy Dressing. Serves 4.

Sesame Soy Dressing

1/4 cup soy sauce

1/4 cup sesame oil

1 cup canola or vegetable oil

1 teaspoon ginger

1 teaspoon pepper

1 tablespoon sugar

Combine all ingredients in a food processor or blender and process only until emulsified. Yields 1 1/2 cups.

SHRIMP LOUIS

THE INNLET CAFÉ, MAHONE BAY, NS

Jack Sorenson calls this dressing his "traditional Thousand Islands Dressing." Historians claim the original dressing was the creation of the chef of the yacht Louise, which belonged to millionaire George C. Boldt of Thousand Islands' Boldt Castle fame. Whatever the source, this version is great!

1 cup egg-based mayonnaise

1/4 cup heavy cream (35% m.f.)

1/4 cup chili sauce

1/4 cup green onion, minced

1 1/2 teaspoon lemon juice

Shredded lettuce to serve 4

1/2 pound large shrimp, cooked and shelled

1/2 pound baby shrimp, cooked and shelled

8 radish, thinly sliced

1/2 English cucumber, thinly sliced

12 black olives

2 hard-boiled eggs, sliced

Blend together mayonnaise, cream, chili sauce, green onion and lemon juice. Spoon sauce over individual beds of shredded lettuce. Embed shrimp in sauce and serve garnished with thinly sliced radish, cucumber, black olives and hard-boiled eggs. Serves 4.

ONTARIO GREENS WITH CARROTS AND BEETS, THYME AND GARLIC DRESSING

THE BRIARS RESORT, JACKSON'S POINT, ON

Chef Trevor Ledlie of the Briars advises that "Ontario Greens" are best described as Cookstown greens, however, any local greens which include sweet and bitter types may be used. He notes that roasting garlic produces a sweet nutty flavour, making the garlic soft and spreadable. Interestingly, the carrot and beet slices quickly blanch as they are submerged in the boiling pickling mixture.

1 small carrot, peeled and thinly sliced

2 baby beets, peeled, and thinly sliced

1 cup water

1 cup white wine vinegar

1 tablespoon pickling spice

1/2 cup sugar

Mixed greens to serve 4 - 6

Thyme and Garlic dressing, recipe follows

Prepare carrot and beets and set aside. In a saucepan bring water, vinegar, pickling spice and sugar to a full boil. Quickly strain mixture and divide between two separate bowls, adding carrot slices to one and beet slices to the other. Cover, allow to cool, then refrigerate several hours.

To serve arrange greens on serving plates, and drizzle with dressing. Drain carrot and beet slices and sprinkle on top. Yields 4 - 6 servings.

Thyme and Garlic Dressing

1/2 cup white wine vinegar

1 tablespoon lemon juice

2 teaspoons fresh thyme, chopped

1-2 cloves roasted garlic, recipe follows

3/4 teaspoon honey

1 1/2 cups olive oil

salt and pepper, to taste

In a food processor or blender combine vinegar, lemon juice, thyme, garlic and honey. With mixer running, add oil in a slow stream, processing until emulsified. Season with salt and pepper and refrigerate.

To Roast Garlic *(supplied by author)*

Preheat oven to 325°F. Lightly coat one whole unpeeled garlic bulb or individual unpeeled cloves with a little olive oil and bake until browned and softened. Allow approximately 30 minutes for the cloves and 45 minutes for the whole garlic bulb. Gently squeeze garlic out of its peel with your fingers.

SMOKED SALMON NAPOLEON SALAD

ARBOR VIEW INN, LUNENBURG, NS

Beautiful in its presentation, this layered salad is the creation of innkeeper chef Daniel Orovec. He suggests that additional tomatoes or latticed potato wafers could be used instead of cucumbers. He insists that only a good quality smoked salmon be used.

1 English cucumber, sliced

1 large bunch watercress

1 large bunch chervil

8-10 ounces thinly sliced smoked salmon

2 large vine-ripened tomatoes, sliced

Infused Basil Oil, recipe follows

fresh thyme or chives, to garnish

In the centre of 2 salad plates arrange rounds of cucumber, overlapping slightly. Top with a few sprigs of watercress and chervil, then add a few slices of smoked salmon. Top again with cucumber, greens, and tomato, followed by more smoked salmon. Finish plate with another layer of greens and salmon. Garnish with thyme or chives, and drizzle with infused basil oil. Serves 2.

Infused Basil Oil

2 cups extra virgin olive oil

1 cup fresh basil leaves, rinsed

In a small saucepan gently warm olive oil, being careful not to bring to a boil. Add basil leaves, remove from heat and let cool. Gently strain oil into a sterilized jar and refrigerate.

TROPICAL CAESAR

LITTLE SHEMOQUE COUNTRY INN, PORT ELGIN, NB

Variations of the classic Caesar salad are too numerous to count. I'm sure you will find this Tropical Caesar a delight — perfect for a warm summer evening!

1/2 romaine lettuce, in bite sized pieces

1 banana, sliced

2 slices pineapple

3/4 cup red seedless grapes

1 7-ounce can water packed solid white tuna

1 tablespoon slivered almonds

Tropical Caesar Dressing, recipe follows

Wash, dry and tear lettuce leaves into bite-sized pieces and mound on 2 serving plates. Place drained tuna in the centre, surround with banana slices, pineapple slices and grapes. Drizzle with dressing and sprinkle with almonds.

Tropical Caesar Dressing

3 tablespoons sour cream

1 1/2 tablespoons mango chutney

1 teaspoon curry

In a small bowl blend dressing ingredients together with a whisk. Refrigerate until serving. Yields 1/2 cup.

Each layer is a gourmet's delight in Smoked Salmon Napoleon ▶ Salad from the Arbor Inn, Lunenburg, NS

CLEOPATRA'S SALAD

MADELYN'S BISTRO, LUNENBURG, NS

Madelyn's Bistro is situated close to the shores of the Atlantic where chef Darrin Myra has fittingly created this seafood Caesar. I feel it is fit for an emperor, or perhaps his lady!

romaine lettuce, to serve 4

Caesar salad dressing of your choice

1/2 red pepper, in julienne strips

1/2 green pepper, in julienne strips

6–8 mushrooms, sliced

1 large tomato, diced

4 large radishes

3 tablespoons butter

1/8 teaspoon dried rosemary, crumbled

1 clove garlic, finely minced

12 tiger shrimp

12 sea scallops

20 mussels

2 tablespoons sherry, slightly warmed

2 slices bacon, cooked crisp and crumbled, as garnish

croutons, as garnish

freshly grated parmesan cheese, as garnish

Prepare romaine and toss with Caesar salad dressing of your choice. Divide between 4 salad plates. Top salads with peppers, mushroom slices, tomatoes and radish.

Melt butter in a sauté pan over medium high heat. Sprinkle shrimps and scallops with rosemary and garlic then quickly saute 3–4 minutes until seafood is just cooked. Remove pan from burner, add slightly warmed sherry and flambé.

While shrimp and scallops are being sautéed steam mussels until shells open and mussels are cooked, approximately 6 minutes.

To serve, top salads with shrimp and scallops, and place mussels in their shells around the edge of the plate. Sprinkle with bacon bits, croutons and parmesan cheese. Drizzle with additional dressing, if desired.

Yields 4 servings

Served with crusty bread, Cleopatra's Salad is a fulfilling meal ▶

THAI CHICKEN SALAD

SUNSHINE ON MAIN CAFÉ & BISTRO, ANTIGONISH, NS

It is, of course, the ingredients in this salad dressing that produces its distinctive flavour. Chef Mark Gabrieau advises that red chili paste and fish sauce or nam pla are available in the speciality section of large supermarkets, Asian markets and imported food stores.

1 large romaine lettuce, in bite-sized pieces

3–4 small cooked chicken breasts, thinly sliced

2 tomatoes, cut in wedges

1/2 English-style cucumber, sliced

1/2 each red and green pepper, julienned

1/2 red onion, thinly sliced

12 small cauliflower fleurettes

Thai Dressing, recipe follows

1 lemon, cut in wedges, as garnish

Prepare romaine and divide between 4 salad plates. Top each salad with a generous portion of sliced chicken, tomato, cucumber, peppers, onion and cauliflower. Drizzle with Thai Dressing and serve, garnished with a lemon wedge.

Serves 4.

Thai Dressing

1 egg

1 cup vegetable oil

1 tablespoon garlic paste or 3 cloves, finely minced

1 tablespoon red chili paste or 2 small chili peppers, minced

generous grinding of black pepper

1 tablespoon freshly chopped mint

1 tablespoons fish sauce (*nam pla*)

1/2 tablespoon champagne vinegar

2 teaspoons freshly chopped cilantro

In a food processor or blender whip egg. With motor running, slowly add oil in a steady stream, processing until mixture becomes the consistency of mayonnaise. Add remaining ingredients and stir to blend well.

A spicy and innovative salad from the Sunshine on Main Café and Bistro, Antigonish, NS ▶

BABY SPINACH SALAD WITH GRILLED SCALLOPS AND ROASTED BEETS

THE HALLIBURTON HOUSE INN, HALIFAX, NS

Halliburton House Inn's chef, Scott Vail, serves this substantial salad to guests when garden beets are at their peak. I suggest you preparethe beets early in the day to allow time for them to cook and cool.

4 small beets, golden or red

pinch each of salt and pepper

1 tablespoon rice wine vinegar

1 tablespoon olive oil

1 1/2 tablespoons olive oil, second amount

12 medium-size sea scallops

1 pound baby spinach, washed, dried and stemmed

Raspberry Walnut Vinaigrette, recipe follows

2 tablespoons cold butter

Preheat oven to 350°F.

Wash beets, season with salt and pepper and toss with rice vinegar and olive oil. Place beets in a covered pan and bake until barely fork tender, approximately 35-45 minutes. Remove from oven and cool, reserving braising liquid. When cool enough to handle, rub off skins and cut each beet into three wedges. Set aside.

Heat a heavy bottomed skillet over high heat. Add second amount of olive oil and sear scallops until just cooked. Remove from burner and keep warm.

To assemble salads, place prepared spinach in a large salad bowl and toss with Raspberry Walnut Vinaigrette. Divide between 4 salad plates. Place three scallops symmetrically on each plate. Place one beet wedge in the space between the scallops. Quickly bring the reserved beet braising liquid to a boil and whisk in the cold butter. Drizzle a ribbon of this liquid around each plate. Serves 4.

Raspberry Walnut Vinaigrette

3 tablespoons raspberry vinegar

1 tablespoon fresh tarragon, finely chopped

1/2 cup walnut oil

salt and pepper, to taste

Using a glass bowl and a wire whisk, mix raspberry vinegar and tarragon. Slowly add walnut oil as you continue to whisk until dressing is emulsified. Season with salt and pepper.

A delicious dish, combining succulent scallops and the rich flavour ▶ of roasted beets, from the Haliburton House Inn, Halifax , NS

WARM SALAD OF BRAISED DUCK

DALVAY-BY-THE-SEA, DALVAY, PEI

*Chef Keith Wilson of Dalvay presents his salad on a toasted round of brioche,
a classic French loaf made with eggs and butter. For the home cook, I suggest you
serve the salad on a round of toast of your choice.*

1 tablespoon vegetable oil

4 duck legs

1 small carrot, pared and coarsely chopped

1 stalk celery, chopped

1 medium onion, chopped

2 cloves garlic, minced

4 cups chicken stock

1 bunch watercress

12 small beets, scrubbed and stalks trimmed

1/4 cup brown sugar

1 teaspoon Dijon mustard

1/4 cup raspberry vinegar

1/4 cup olive oil

1/4 cup walnut oil

salt and pepper, to taste

4 round slices of toast

1/4 cup walnuts, chopped

Preheat oven to 325°F.

Heat oil in an oven proof skillet over medium heat and gently brown duck legs, turning as necessary. Remove duck and reserve. Add carrot, celery, onion and garlic to pan and sauté until lightly browned. Place duck legs on top of vegetable mixture, add stock and cover with foil.

Duck legs should be almost submerged in the stock. Braise in oven for 2 hours.

When meat is cool enough to handle, remove meat from the bone and set aside.

Prepare watercress by trimming stems, rinse and spin dry, then refrigerate. Place prepared beets on a baking sheet, cover with foil and bake at 325°F for approximately 3/4 hour until soft. Remove skins, placing beets to one side. Place beet skins and one coarsely chopped beet into a saucepan. Barely cover with water, add brown sugar; boil and reduce until a syrup is formed.

Strain syrup into a food processor. Add mustard and vinegar, then process. Combine oils in a small carafe, then with processor running, add in a slow steady stream. Season with salt and pepper.

To assemble, toast 4 slices of white bread, cut into round discs and place in the centre of each plate. Arrange beets and walnuts around the edge. Drizzle dressing over beets. Top toast with watercress and pieces of warm duck. Serves 4.

Warm Salad of Braised Duck from chef Keith Wilson at Dalvay-by-the-Sea, Dalvay, PEI ▶

CHICKEN LIVER FLAMBÉ IN BRANDY ON BELGIAN ENDIVE

LITTLE SHEMOQUE COUNTRY INN, PORT ELGIN, NB

*Innkeeper Petra Sudbrack occasionally has guests arrive past the set dinner hour.
She serves them this innovative and filling salad, thus presenting a "preview"
of the wonderful cuisine of the inn.*

2 Belgium endive

2 cups assorted greens

2 tablespoons butter

3 small garlic cloves, minced

20 chicken livers, approximately 1/2 pound

sprigs fresh rosemary

salt and black pepper, to taste

2 tablespoons brandy

20 blossoms, e.g. nasturtium, pansy,
marigold, etc.

Dressing, recipe follows

Dressing

6 tablespoons olive oil

2 tablespoons red wine vinegar

1 teaspoon Dijon mustard

1 small garlic clove, finely minced

salt and freshly grated black pepper, to taste

Whisk together all ingredients in a small bowl
until emulsified. Yields 1/2 cup.

Divide endive into individual leaves, allowing
5 large leaves per plate. Chop additional
leaves and mix with salad greens, if desired.

Melt the butter in a sauté pan over medium
high heat. Quickly sauté the garlic and livers,
allowing 2 minutes per side. Remove pan
from burner and flambé with brandy.

To serve, arrange five endive leaves in the
shape of a star, per salad plate. Place salad
greens between endive and top each endive
leaf with a sautéed chicken liver. Decorate
plates with blossoms and drizzle with dressing.

Serves 4.

*This Chicken Liver Flambé is the creation of Petra Sudbrack at the ▶
Little Shemogne Country Inn, Port Elgin, NB*

SALAD OF SAUTÉED LOBSTER WITH LOBSTER OIL VINAIGRETTE

SEASONS IN THYME, SUMMERSIDE, PEI

Seasons in Thyme Restaurant epitomizes what is innovative in Canadian cuisine. Owner-chef Stephan Czapalay has developed a marvellous product in his kitchen called Canadian Cold Water Lobster Oil. This recipe uses his lobster oil, which is available from the restaurant, but he advises that any flavoured oil may be substituted.

1 tablespoon butter

1 teaspoon Canadian Cold Water Lobster Oil

12 ounces lobster meat

4 cups mesclun greens

4 sheets dried nori*, 3 x 12 inches

Lobster Oil Vinaigrette, recipe follows

4 teaspoons black sesame seeds

Over medium heat combine butter and oil and sauté lobster for about 3 minutes.

To serve, toss greens with a small amount of vinaigrette and divide between 4 individual plates. If nori sheets are brittle, refresh with cold water until pliable. Wrap greens in small bundles with the nori. Divide lobster pieces between salads, decoratively drizzle plates with a little vinaigrette and sprinkle with sesame seeds. Serves 4.

* Nori are paper thin sheets of dried seaweed, ranging in colour from green to purple to black. It is available in Asian or speciality food stores.

Lobster Oil Vinaigrette

1/4 cup olive oil

1/4 cup Canadian Cold Water Lobster Oil

1 1/2 teaspoons sesame oil

1/4 cup melfour vinegar*

In a small bowl whisk together the olive oil, lobster oil, sesame oil and vinegar.

* If melfour vinegar is unavailable substitute an equal amount of maple vinegar or cider vinegar plus 1 teaspoon liquid honey.

An elegant and impressive offering from Seasons in Thyme, Summerside, PEI ▶

SALAD OF GOAT CHEESE, NASTURTIUM AND POACHED PLUMS

INN AT BAY FORTUNE, BAY FORTUNE, PEI

Always creative, chef Michael Smith suggests you prepare this colourful salad when your summer flowers are at their peak. You may watch Smith weekly on Life Channel TV as he energetically stars in his program "Inn Chef"

1 tablespoon Dijon mustard

1 tablespoon liquid honey

1 tablespoon white wine vinegar

3 tablespoons extra virgin olive oil

pinch of salt

freshly ground black pepper

3–4 cups nasturtium leaves and flowers

4 cheese balls, recipe follows

4 poached plums, recipe follows

Whisk together the mustard, honey, vinegar, oil and seasonings.

To serve, toss the nasturtiums with vinaigrette and divide between four plates. Top each salad with a warm cheese ball, poached plum and a decorative cracker. Serves 4.

Cheese Balls

12 ounces fresh goat cheese, softened

2 tablespoons chives, finely sliced

1/2 teaspoon freshly ground pepper

1 tablespoon nasturtium flowers, chopped

1/2 cup flour

2 eggs

2 tablespoons water

1 cup ground walnuts

In a stainless steel bowl mix together cheese, chives, pepper and nasturtium flowers until thoroughly blended. Form into 4 evenly shaped balls. Place balls in the refrigerator until firm, about 1 hour. Roll refrigerated balls in flour.

In a small bowl whisk together eggs and water. Dip cheese balls in egg wash, then roll in crushed nuts. Return to the freezer to thoroughly chill.

Preheat oven to 400° F.

Bake the cheese balls for about 5 minutes, just long enough to set the outer crust and warm the cheese.

Poached Plums

1 cup Port wine

1 cup sugar

1/2 teaspoon freshly ground black pepper

4 ripe plums

Place wine, sugar and pepper in a small saucepan and simmer 5 minutes, then add the plums. Simmer for 5 minutes, remove from heat and allow to rest in the syrup for 12 hours.

Make a small incision in the blossom end of the plum and remove the pit at serving time.

Salad of Goat Cheese Nasturtium and Poached Plums from Inn at Bay Fortune, Bay Fortune, PEI ▶

SALAD OF ASPARAGUS, ARTICHOKES AND CRISP PROSCIUTTO

DALVAY-BY-THE-SEA, DALVAY, PEI

Chef Keith Wilson of Dalvay-by-the-Sea prepares his Parmesan Oil Dressing and salad vegetables early in the day. At serving time he simply fries the artichokes and prosciutto, then serves this beautiful warm salad.

1/4 pound fresh parmesan cheese (with rind)

2/3 cup extra virgin olive oil

4 shallots

1 can water-packed artichoke hearts, 14-ounce size

1 red pepper

16 fresh asparagus spears

2 tablespoons raspberry vinegar

1/4 teaspoon grain mustard

salt and pepper, to taste

8 thin slices prosciutto

2 chives, chopped

Cut rind from parmesan and reserve. Shave parmesan with a vegetable parer and refrigerate. Place olive oil and parmesan rind into a saucepan. Over a gentle heat warm oil and rind slightly. Set aside at room temperature for at least 6 hours to allow flavours to infuse. Remove rind.

Peel shallots and slice into 3 slices. Place face down in a skillet, drizzle with a little infused oil and sauté over very low heat until shallots are soft and golden in colour. Remove from heat and allow to cool.

Drain artichokes, cut in half length-wise and pat dry. Drizzle with a little infused oil, allowing just enough to provide a thin coating, set aside.

Preheat oven to 350°F. Lightly coat red pepper in oil, place in a baking pan and cover with foil. Bake approximately 20 minutes, turning occasionally until pepper is soft and skin is blistered. Remove from pan and put into a bowl, cover with plastic wrap. When cool, remove seeds and skin and slice pepper into strips.

Using a vegetable peeler, gently remove tough skin from the stalk of asparagus. Boil asparagus for approximately 1 1/2 minutes, then plunge into cold water to stop cooking process and retain colour. The asparagus should be cooked but crisp. Pat dry with paper towel and set aside.

Combine vinegar and mustard in a bowl. Add remaining oil and whisk until emulsified. Season with salt and pepper.

To serve, fry artichokes and prosciutto in a non-stick fry pan until artichokes are golden brown and prosciutto is crisp.

Assemble by dividing asparagus, shaved parmesan, shallots and red peppers between four plates. Drizzle with parmesan oil. Arrange warm artichokes and prosciutto over vegetables and sprinkle with chopped chives. Serves 4.

Salad of Asparagus Artichokes and Crisp Prosciutto from ▶ chef Keith Wilson at Dalvay-by-the-Sea

INDEX